SS

D0575501

DATE DUE

What's Inside Me?
My Skin

Dana Meachen Rau

BENCHMARK **B**OOKS

MARSHALL CAVENDISH
NEW YORK

My Skin

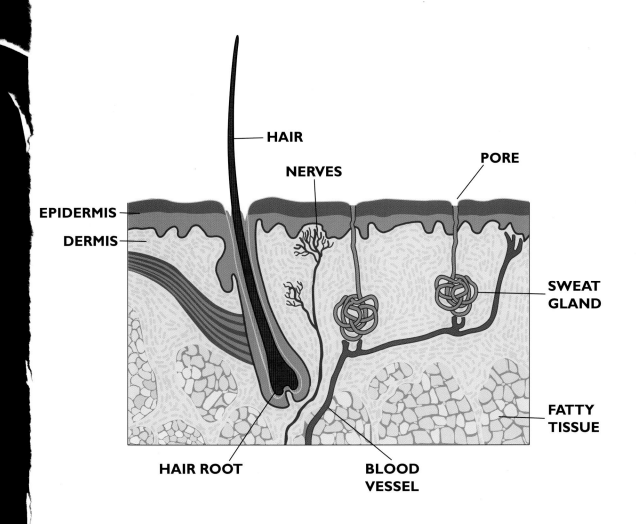

HAIR

NERVES

PORE

EPIDERMIS

DERMIS

SWEAT
GLAND

HAIR ROOT

BLOOD
VESSEL

FATTY
TISSUE

There is a lot going on inside your body. Your body is filled with blood, bones, and *organs*.

All your organs have important jobs to do. Your lungs help you breathe. Your heart pumps your blood.

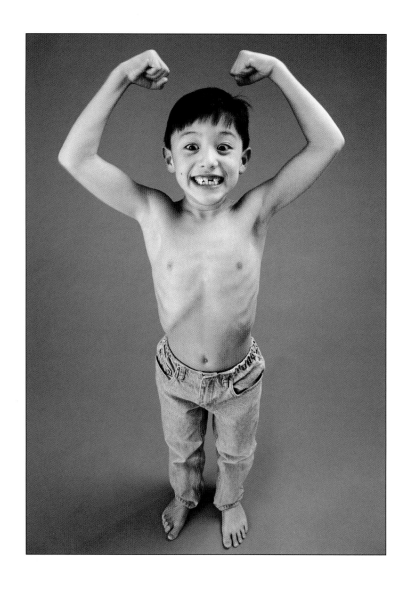

Your skin is your largest organ. It covers your whole body. It is in charge of protecting all your inside parts.

Germs are all around us.
Germs can make you sick.
Your skin keeps germs out
of your body.

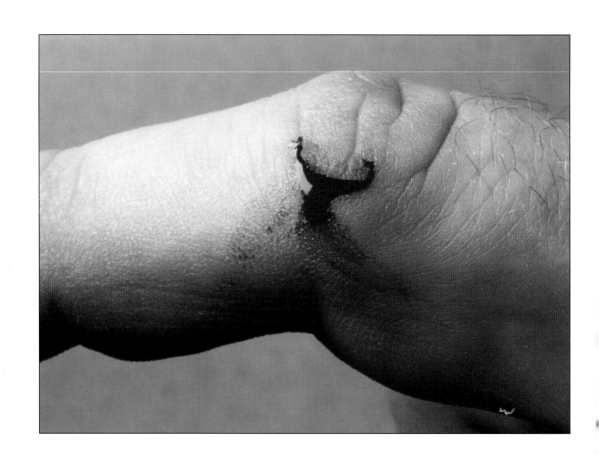

Germs can get into a cut in your skin.

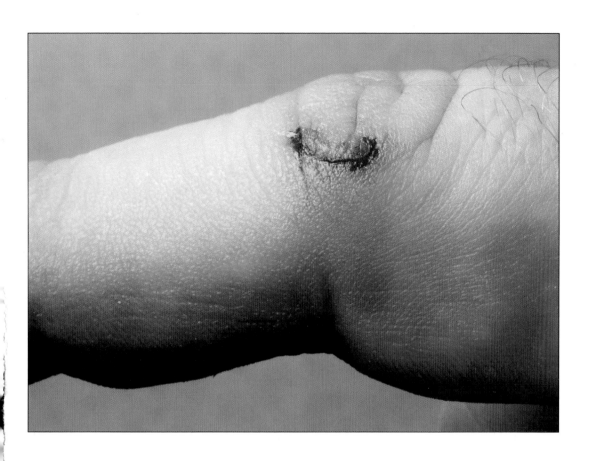

Blood forms a scab to plug up
the cut and keep the germs out.

The skin you see on the outside of your body is called your *epidermis*. Your epidermis is made up of tiny *cells*.

The cells of your epidermis are dead. Millions of these dry dead cells fall off your body every day.

There is another layer of skin under the epidermis. This living inside layer is called the *dermis*. It makes millions of new skin cells every day.

The dermis is filled with little tubes that carry blood. These tubes are called *blood vessels*.

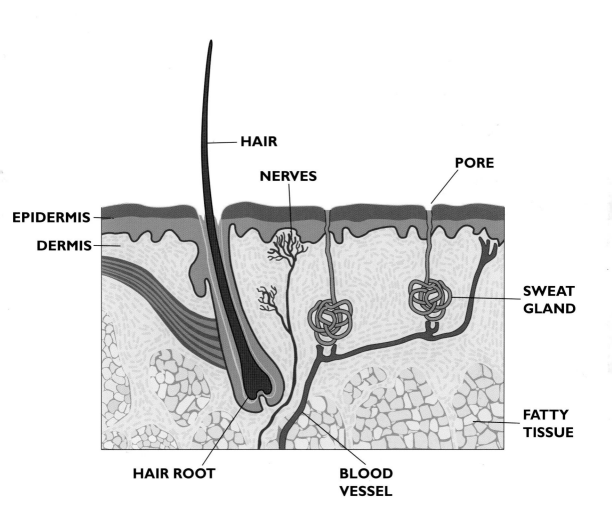

HAIR

NERVES

PORE

EPIDERMIS

DERMIS

SWEAT
GLAND

HAIR ROOT

BLOOD
VESSEL

FATTY
TISSUE

15

Your dermis also has *nerves*.
Nerves help you feel if something
is rough or smooth.

They help you feel if something is hot or cold.

Your skin is covered with tiny hairs. Only the palms of your hands and the bottoms of your feet do not have hair.

The roots of the hair are deep in the dermis. The roots are alive. But the hair outside the skin is dead.

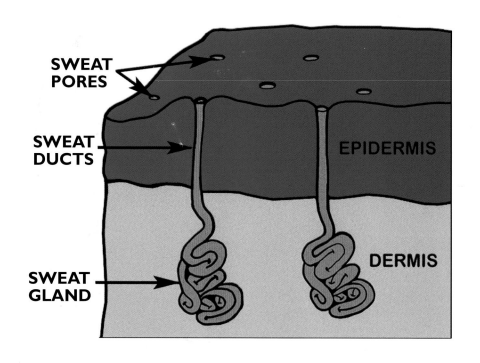

SWEAT PORES

SWEAT DUCTS

EPIDERMIS

SWEAT GLAND

DERMIS

Your skin is filled with *sweat glands*. Sweat comes out of the sweat glands through a hole in your skin. This hole is called a *pore*.

Sweating keeps your body cool when you get hot.

All people have different colored skin. *Melanin* gives skin its color.

People with dark skin have a lot of melanin. People with light skin have just a little.

Freckles are spots with a lot of melanin.

The sun makes your skin create more melanin. If you have light skin and sit outside in the sun, your skin might get darker. This is called tanning.

But the sun can hurt your skin, too. Sunburn makes your skin turn red.

The top layer of your skin may peel, and your skin will sting.

Your skin protects you. It is important for you to protect your skin, too.

Challenge Words

blood vessels—Little tubes that carry blood.

cells (SELLS)—The tiniest building blocks of life that make up all living things.

dermis (DUHR-muhs)—The living inside layer of skin.

epidermis (eh-puh-DUHR-muhs)—The dead outer layer of skin.

germs—Something that can make you sick.

melanin (MEH-luh-nin)—The material that gives skin color.

nerves—Wire-like cords that run to all parts of your body.

organs—Parts of your body with special jobs.

pore—A tiny hole in your skin that lets out sweat.

sweat glands—Tubes deep in the dermis that make sweat.

Index

Page numbers in **boldface** are illustrations.

With thanks to Nanci Vargus, Ed.D. and Beth Walker Gambro, reading consultants

Benchmark Books
Marshall Cavendish
99 White Plains Road
Tarrytown, New York 10591-9001
www.marshallcavendish.com

Text copyright © 2005 by Marshall Cavendish Corporation

Library of Congress Cataloging-in-Publication Data

Rau, Dana Meachen, 1971–
My skin / by Dana Meachen Rau.
p. cm. — (Bookworms: What's inside me?)
Includes index.
ISBN 0-7614-1778-8
1. Skin—Juvenile literature. I. Title. II. Series.

QP88.5.R38 2004
612.7'9—dc22
2004003056

Photo Research by Anne Burns Images

Cover Photo by *Corbis*/Royalty Free

The photographs in this book are used with the permission and through the courtesy of:
Corbis: pp. 1, 23 Laura Doss; p. 2 Anthony Nex; pp. 5, 9 Royalty Free; p. 6 Luis Pelaez; p. 12 Rob & Sas;
p. 16 Tom Stewart; p. 17 Ed Bock; p. 19 L. Clarke; p. 21 Tim Pannell; p. 24 Wartenberg/Picture Press;
p. 27 Bohemian Nomad Picturemakers; p. 28 Ariel Skelley. *Photo Researchers*: pp. 10, 11 Eric Schrempp.
Custom Medical Stock Photo: p. 20.

Series design by Becky Terhune
Illustrations by Ian Warpole

Printed in China
1 3 5 6 4 2